WALKER BOOKS
AND SUBSIDIARIES
LONDON · BOSTON · SYDNEY · AUCKLAND

First published 2021 by Walker Books Ltd, 87 Vauxhall Walk, London SE11 5HJ · This edition published 2022 · 10 9 8 7 6 5 4 3 2 1
Text © 2021 Martin Jenkins · Illustrations © 2021 Jane McGuinness · The right of Martin Jenkins and Jane McGuinness to be identified as author and
illustrator respectively of this work has been asserted by them in accordance with the Copyright, Designs and Patents Act 1988 · This work has been
typeset in HVD Bodedo and Hammersmith One · Printed in China · All rights reserved. No part of this book may be reproduced, transmitted or stored in
an information retrieval system in any form or by any means, graphic, electronic or mechanical, including photocopying, taping and recording, without
prior written permission from the publisher · British Library Cataloguing in Publication Data: a catalogue record for this book is available from the
British Library · ISBN 978-1-5295-0384-5 · www.walker.co.uk

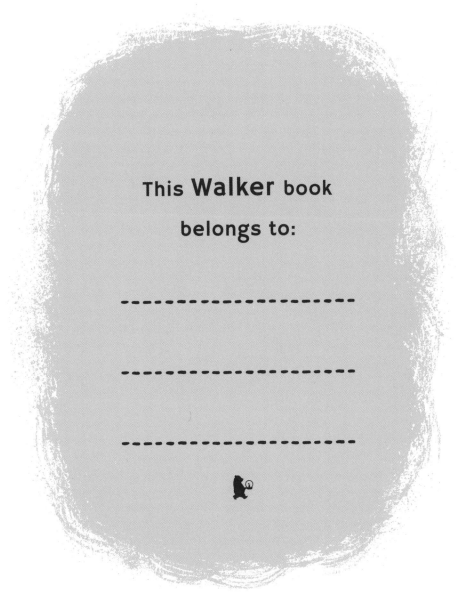

This **Walker** book
belongs to:

FIND OUT ABOUT
Animal Homes

illustrated by

Martin Jenkins

Jane McGuinness

Lots of different kinds of animal make a home to live in. They make them for all sorts of reasons: to stay warm and dry when it's cold and wet outside, as somewhere safe to look after their babies, and to protect themselves from other animals that might eat them.
Here are some of the homes that animals make...

There are **big** animals that have small **homes.**

A mother polar bear digs a cosy den in the snow just big enough for her and her cubs. It's warm and snug in there while it's freezing outside.

And small animals that have **big** homes, with air-conditioning and everything.

Termites live underground at the bottom of their mound. Most kinds of termite are smaller than your little fingernail, but they can build mounds as tall as a bus – though it takes millions of them to do it! The way the mound is made keeps the air inside cool and fresh.

There are animals that make their
homes out of sticks.

Lots of different kinds of bird make nests out of sticks to lay their eggs in. Storks make especially big nests. Often one pair uses the same nest year after year.

And ones that make them out of stones.

Young caddisflies, called larvae, live underwater. Some of them build homes out of tiny stones glued together with sticky stuff called silk that they make themselves. Each larva carries its home around with it.

And even some that make them out of spit. Yuk!

Edible-nest swiftlets live in Asia. They use their own saliva, or spit, to make nests.
The saliva hardens to make a safe place for the swiftlets' eggs and chicks.

There are animals that build homes
that last for years and years.

Prairie dogs live in big underground towns made of tunnels which they dig themselves.
The tunnels have rooms for sleeping, bringing up babies and going to the toilet.
The towns can be dozens of kilometres long and
hundreds of years old.

And animals that build
a new one every day.

Each evening an orangutan makes a
comfortable nest out of branches and leaves
to sleep in that night. Sometimes
they'll build one for an afternoon
snooze as well!

Honeybees fill their hives with little cells made from beeswax to lay their eggs in. The cells are all exactly the same size and fit together with no spaces between them.

There are animals with beautifully neat and tidy homes.

And animals with messy ones (like me!).

Pack rats build their nests out of all sorts of stuff - mostly rubbish
like sticks, stones, plastic pots, rusty wire and old bones.

There are animals with homes
that make a big impression.

Beavers dam up rivers and streams with mud, stones and trees that they cut down. This creates big ponds that they build their dens, called lodges, in.

And animals with homes that you can hardly see.

Some spiders build underground tunnels hidden beneath a trapdoor. When a small animal such as a cricket passes by, the spider pushes open the door and leaps out to grab it.

And there are quite a lot of animals that don't make homes at all, but seem perfectly happy wherever they happen to be!

Reindeer live in the snowy north. They go on long journeys to escape the coldest part of the winter. Some of them walk over 4,000 kilometres every year!

More about animals and their homes:

Most animals spend their lives living in one particular place that they know well, called a territory – it's their home. They know where to find food, and where they can hide from animals that might hunt them. Often they try to keep other animals of the same kind away.

Animals sometimes change their territories to make life safer for themselves. Often they dig burrows there to hide away in. But the commonest thing that animals do is build a nest, where they can look after their babies when they are young. Most birds do this. A lot of insects, like termites and bees, make homes for their young too. Different insects use different things to make their homes. Honeybees make their own beeswax. Termites mostly use their own poo! They mix it with sand and spit so that it sets hard like concrete.

Not all animals have territories or homes. Animals that don't, like reindeer, usually live in big groups and travel about from place to place looking for food. They often come back to the same places year after year. Perhaps when they return they recognize them and think of them as a kind of home too.

INDEX